HERBAL WREATHS

More Than 60 Fragrant,
Colorful Wreaths to Make and Enjoy

CAROL TAYLOR

Watercolors by Diane Weaver

A Sterling/Lark Book
Sterling Publishing Co., Inc.   New York

Art Directors: Sandra Montgomery, Marcia Winters
Photography: Evan Bracken
Production: Sandra Montgomery, Elaine Thompson

Library of Congress Cataloging-in-Publication Data
Taylor, Carol, [date]
  Herbal wreaths : more than 60 fragrant, colorful wreaths to
make and enjoy / Carol Taylor ; watercolors by Diane Weaver.
     p.   cm.
  "A Sterling/Lark book."
  Includes index.
  ISBN 0-8069-8600-X
  1. Wreaths.   2. Herbs—Utilization.   3. Herb gardening.
I. Title
SB449.5.W74T38   1992
745.92--dc20   91-33467
                                                CIP

ISBN 0-8069-8600-X Trade
       0-8069-8601-8 Paper

10 9 8 7 6 5 4 3 2 1

A Sterling/Lark Book

Produced by Altamont Press, Inc.
50 College St., Asheville, NC 28801

Published in 1992 by Sterling Publishing Co., Inc.
387 Park Ave. S., New York, NY 10016

© 1992, Altamont Press

Distributed in Canada by Sterling Publishing,
c/o Canadian Manda Group, P.O. Box 920, Station U, Toronto,
   Ontario M8Z 5P9
Distributed in the United Kingdom by Cassell PLC, Villiers House,
   41/47 Strand, London WC2N 5JE, England
Distributed in Australia by Capricorn Link Ltd., P.O. Box 665,
   Lane Cove, NSW 2066

Every effort has been made to ensure that all information in this
book is accurate. However, due to differing conditions, tools,
and individual skills, the publisher cannot be responsible for any
injuries, losses, or other damages which may result from the use
of the information in this book.

Printed in Hong Kong

Contributing Designers

Barbara Applebaum, together with her husband Lewis, owns and operates Brush Creek Farms in Fairview, North Carolina. Using organic growing methods, they cultivate over 300 different herbs. (Pages 34, 36, 46, 52, 54, and 90.)

Nora Blose learned to value herbs when her aunt, a country doctor, treated her patients with herbal medicines. Nora lives in Enka, North Carolina, where she makes and markets herbal crafts. (Pages 14, 28, 32, 60, 86, 94, 106, and 108.)

Janet Frye is the proprietor of The Enchanted Florist in Arden, North Carolina. An award-winning designer, Janet has been a florist for 15 years and has taught design for eight. (Pages 18, 37, 53, 56, 83, 104, 105, and 110.)

Jeannette Hafner grows the flowers and greenery for her designs in her gardens in Orange, Connecticut. She teaches drying and arranging techniques as well as design classes. (Pages 44, 47, and 71.)

Alyce Nadeau grows 200 different herbs for her business, Goldenrod Mountain Herbs, in Deep Gap, North Carolina. She has been known to arrange an herbal wedding, complete with food, beverage, wreaths, and bouquets.

(The front cover and pages 19, 20, 58, 76, 80, 100, and 102.)

Alan Salmon owns and operates Wildwood Herbal Flower Farm at Reems Creek, in Weaverville, North Carolina, with his wife Betty Sparrow. They started an herb cooperative with members throughout Western North Carolina. (Pages 23, 74, and 111 bottom left.)

Beth Stickle is the proprietor of Bloomin' Art in Asheville, North Carolina, where she designs and sells floral and herbal crafts. (Pages 40, 43, 57, 77, 82, and 111 top.)

Sylvia Tippitt owns and operates Rasland Farms in Godwin, North Carolina. On her eight-acre herb farm she cultivates herbs both common and obscure, and sells both herbs and crafts through mail order. (Pages 4, 16, and 50.)

Diane Weaver worked as an art director/designer in Detroit and New York. With husband Dick, she operates Gourmet Gardens, an herb nursery in Weaverville, North Carolina. (The back cover and pages 13, 22, 24, 26, 30, 38, 42, 48, 66, 70, 72, 78, 84, 88, 92, 93, 96, and 98.)

And thanks to . . .
Dawn Cusick (page 62), Cynthia Gillooley (page 3), Bessie Smith (page 68), and Gail Wynne (64).

3

Introduction
• 6 •

The Basics of Wreath Making
Herbs, Wreath Bases, Means of Attachment, Wreath Design
• 8 •

Herbal Wreaths

Index
• 112 •

Introduction

Herbs are like art and obscenity: they're difficult to define, but we know them when we see them. Often herbs are defined as "useful plants"—which is perhaps a redundancy. After all, in this age of greenhouse gases, what oxygen-producing, carbon-dioxide-consuming stalk of greenery is *not* useful?

More particularly, herbs are plants that have had a special relationship to humanity since before recorded history—plants that have healed our wounds, moderated our illnesses, seasoned our food, scented our homes, driven off our demons, and brought beauty and grace to our lives.

Like other plants, herbs speak to us of sun and rain and earth. Even more, they speak to us of belonging. If even the weeds that grow wild on this Planet Earth can bring us health and nourishment and joy, then surely we must be welcome here. Surely we are at home.

Even after all these centuries, we are still finding new uses for herbs. One of the most delightful is an herbal wreath. Wreath making is a simple process that yields disproportionately satisfying results. However you come by your herbs—whether you pick them in a pasture, grow them in your garden, or buy them at a farmer's market—you have only to attach them to a wreath base and hang them on a wall to enjoy their fragrance and beauty.

Eventually you may tire of them. Perhaps one day we will all tire of herbs. But that may take several centuries more.

Left: Purple Coneflowers. Endpapers: Pink Yarrow.

The Basics

To make an herbal wreath, you need three things: herbs, a wreath base, and a way to hold the two together. The rest is creativity.

HERBS

Growing

Herb gardens have become so popular that all major seed companies and decent-sized nurseries carry dozens of varieties. Seed packets and nursery staff are excellent sources of detailed information. In general, herbs like sun and average, well-drained soil. If they're overfed, they'll produce lush growth at the expense of color, scent, and flavor.

Harvesting

Herbs should be harvested on a sunny morning, after the dew has dried and before the sun is hot. As mystical as that sounds, it's purely practical advice. Herbs that are picked wet won't dry as well, and the hot sun causes chemical changes in the plant that diminish its fragrance and color.

Traditional advice is to harvest herbs just before they flower, the point at which the leaves are highest in essential oil and thus most fragrant and flavorful. That advice holds if you're gathering herbs to cook with. For craft purposes, harvest herbs when the foliage and flowers look the way you want them to on the wreath. There's no point in gathering half-open anise hyssop flowers if what you want is the full lavender beauty of the blooms.

Feverfew

Yarrow

Drying

Fresh wreaths are colorful and fragrant—well worth the time required to put them together—but they last only a few days. With dried materials, your wreaths can last for months.

Air-drying. The simplest method is to form loose bunches of six to 10 stems and secure them with string, a rubber band, or even an old twist tie. Then hang the bunches upside down in a warm, dry, dark place—warm and dry so the herbs will release their moisture, dark so sunlight won't leach color, fragrance, and flavor from the plants.

This rules out a sunny window and a steamy kitchen or bathroom. A linen closet, a shady screened porch, a heated guest bedroom with the shades drawn would all work. A few tips:

❖ Don't tie more than six to 10 stems in one bunch. If air can't circulate to the center, the herbs on the inside will mold. In fact, with leaves that are especially "juicy," you might limit the bunches to four or five stems.

❖ How long the herbs will take to dry depends on the herbs and the weather. Herbs that are fairly dry by nature (rosemary, for example) will dry in a few days. Juicier herbs, such as mint, may take two to three weeks. You can tell when they're ready: flowers feel rigid and leaves feel, well, dry. Both will rustle when shaken gently.

❖ When the herbs are dry, move them to a dark, cool place. Overdried herbs are difficult to work with; they tend to shatter upon contact.

Top: Purple Sage. Bottom: Catmint.

Top: Tansy. Bottom: Pineapple Mint.

9

≈ If the herbs are hard to hang—if you're drying flowerheads, for example, or very short-stemmed plants—set a window screen on four flowerpots, and lay the materials on the screen to dry.

Silica gel. This fine powder is the latest in a long line of desiccants—moisture-absorbing substances such as sand and borax that have been used for years. Available wherever craft supplies are sold, silica gel speeds the drying process. Be sure to check the manufacturer's instructions.

In general, pour about an inch (2.5 cm) of gel

into the bottom of a plastic, glass, or metal container (fruitcake tins work well), and lay the herbs on top, leaving space around each one. Cover the plants with more gel. Avoid twisting them into unnatural positions, which may be permanent once they're dry. If they have similar drying times, you can add another layer of herbs and another of gel, continuing until the dish is full.

Drying times vary from a couple of days to a week or longer. Check the herbs every few days. Plants can over-dry in silica gel in nothing flat.

When you remove the dry herbs from the gel, use a small, soft paint brush to brush off any left-over powder sticking to the leaves or petals.

Microwave oven. The quickest way to dry herbs is to cover them in silica gel and zap them in the microwave. Using a non-metal container, prepare the herbs as described above, but use a thin layer of gel under and on top of the herbs. Set the oven on medium (300 to 350 watts), and microwave for 1-1/2 to 2-1/2 minutes, depending on how much gel you're using and the idiosyncrasies of your oven.

Lamb's Ear

Anise Hyssop

10

Let the cooked herbs stand for 10 to 30 minutes, depending on the massiveness of their blooms.

Over the season, experiment with individual herbs in your particular microwave, taking notes on times and results each time you dry.

WREATH BASES

Even discount marts in remote parts of the world carry the most common wreath bases. Craft stores carry additional, even off-beat kinds.

Straw. A straw base is broad and bulky. Whether it's an eight-inch or a 20-inch base (20 or 50 cm), there's a lot of surface to cover on that doughnut. Thus straw bases produce lush, full wreaths, like the basil wreath on page 23. Make sure the base is completely covered. Naked straw is not a pretty sight.

Vine. Vine bases can also support lush foliage and flowers (see the wreath on page 13), but they give you another option. Large or small, vine bases are more delicate. They can handle just a few strands of foliage and look restrained rather than pitiful. (Note the small cat mint wreath on page 32.) Parts of a vine wreath left deliberately bare blend well with herbs and flowers, sort of one plant to another.

Wire rings. Whether it's a purchased base or a coat hanger formed into a circle, wire rings are excellent bases for delicate wreaths. Form a mini bouquet of foliage and attach it to the ring by wrapping monofilament (fishing line) or floral wire around the stems and the ring. Lay another bunch on top of the first, and wire that one on the same way. Continue around the ring until it's covered. The artemisias are excellent for this purpose.

Foam. Rigid plastic foam is wonderfully lightweight and available almost everywhere. Covered with moss, it supplies a convenient and inexpensive base.

Also available are rings of wet-type foam, which allow you to construct fresh wreaths. Fine-grained wet foam absorbs and holds moisture, which the plants can use at will. Insert the stems of flowers and foliage directly into the base, and water it every day.

Moss. Wire frames covered with moss are attractive, ready-to-use bases. The heart-shaped wreath on page 100 rests on such a base.

Herb. A woody herb can be shaped into a circle, tied with wire or floral tape, and used as a base. The bee balm wreath on page 28 is simply fresh-cut Scotch broom taped in three places. For the wreath on page 102, the designer made a circle of fresh thyme and wrapped it with monofilament. After drying for a week, it was sturdy enough to support lots of fresh thyme.

Oddball. Even if nobody else thinks of a straw place mat as a wreath base, you can. (The designer of the mint wreath on page 76 did.) Two squares of galvanized wire looked like a base to the maker of the marjoram wreath on page 72. The designer of the eucalyptus wreath on page 42 had a vision of what she wanted in a base. Since no one else shared it, she carved her own out of a piece of plastic foam.

MEANS OF ATTACHMENT

Many of the tools of wreath making have the word "floral" in front of them—floral picks, floral tape, floral pins. That doesn't mean you have to stalk a florist or visit a floral supply house to get them. All these items are available at discount marts and craft stores.

Preliminaries. Two items are absolutely basic.

Floral wire is flexible wire painted green. It comes in straight lengths, in coils, or on spools, and it's available at craft stores in different gauges, or thicknesses. The higher the gauge, the finer the wire. Use a heavier gauge when you need to strengthen a flimsy stem—hold a piece of wire parallel to the stem, and wrap both with floral tape.

Floral tape is less sticky than other types. It adheres to itself (and to other things) when it's stretched. Available in dark green, light green, and brown, it can be selected to match the material you're working with.

Picks. Floral picks are slender pieces of wood with a thin, flexible wire attached to one end. Available in green or natural wood, they're usually three inches or six inches long (7.5 or 15 cm).

To use a floral pick, hold it parallel to the stems of flowers or foliage, and wrap the wire around the stems and the pick itself, starting at the top and spiraling downward. For a secure bond and easy insertion, wrap floral tape around the joined pick and stems.

As you insert picks into a wreath base, make sure that the foliage of the second bunch covers the picked stems of the first, and so on around the wreath. Insert the last pick under the first, and the base will be well covered.

Picks are also useful for odd-shaped items. To attach a deer (okay, a small deer), pull the wire off

the pick and insert the pick into the deer at a strategic location. Or glue a sponge mushroom to a pick, and insert it in the base.

Pins. U-shaped floral pins are decidedly low-tech. They are excellent for attaching background moss

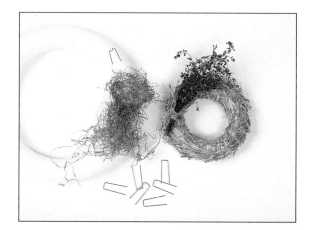

to a base. Many herbal crafters, who often work with bulky foliage, use pins for attaching the herbs themselves. First make bunches of herbs by wrapping the stems with spool-type floral wire, floral tape, or even rubber bands, then pin the mini bouquets on the base.

Hot glue. A glue gun is an indispensable tool for

a wreath maker. Once the herbs are on the base, looking handsome but rather plain, how else are you going to attach the strawflowers or zinnias or globe amaranth that will add color and contrast?

Widely available at discount marts, glue guns heat sticks of glue, liquefying them. The glue coming out of the barrel is, of course, hot. If you find that you burn yourself with some frequency,

check out the warm-melt guns on the market. They use glue that melts at a lower temperature.

DESIGN

Assembling piles of wreath bases, mounds of herbs, and stacks of flowers is one thing. Putting them together into a whole that pleases you is another.

Actually, there's not much to it—just experiment until you get an effect you like. In the absence of inspiration, there are a couple of techniques that wreath makers rely on.

Sectioning. One option is to mentally divide the base into three parts: the inner circle (the "doughnut hole"), the outer circumference of the wreath, and the face. Then you can fill each section separately. For example, the maker of the nigella wreath on page 78 used dark magnolia leaves to establish the inner and outer circles, then covered the face with a variety of materials.

Angles. Consider the angle at which you're attaching materials to the base. One choice is to insert all your materials at the same angle, creating a kind of spiral effect around the base. The lavender wreath on page 68 uses just such a spiral pattern. Alternatively, you can use different angles in different areas. For example, on the lavender wreath on page 70, the designer worked down from the top on each side of the base.

Line. Consider adding a straight line here and there. The designer of the yarrow wreath on page 110 got tired of round—so she added strong vertical and horizontal lines with cinnamon sticks and yarrow stems, for a striking effect.

Color. The only requirement is to have something in mind. Wreaths can look very good with hues of the same general intensity—for example, pale pink flowers on a silver base, page 18—or they can be stunning with contrasting hues (note the vivid wreath at left).

Anise Hyssop

AGASTACHE FOENICULUM

The fragrant lavender blooms of this little-known herb sway gracefully in the lightest breeze. Anise hyssop grows three to four feet tall (just under to just over a meter) and attracts honeybees and butterflies throughout the late summer months. It also attracts crafters. Hung upside down in an airy room, the purple blossoms dry well, retaining their shape and much of their color.

The leaves don't offer much in the way of beauty, but they make an excellent, anise-flavored tea. (Another name for this herb is licorice mint.)

Sow the seeds in spring for a late-summer crop. Anise hyssop likes to be watered and fed, and is thus grateful for mulch.

To make the wreath at left, form mini bouquets of anise hyssop flowers and pick them into a grapevine base, leaving the top bare and adding extra fullness at the bottom. Include an occasional leaf as an accent. Finally, shape mini bouquets of Rose of Sharon blooms, and pick them in at strategic points.

Artemisia

Few herbs are as indispensable to the wreath maker as the artemisias. They're among the most common background materials, partly because their silver foliage complements colorful flowers and herbs, partly because the artemisias grow so prolifically and dry so well that just about everybody has a large supply on hand.

The foliage ranges from moonlight silver to gray green. Silver king (shown in the drawing), silver queen, and silver mound varieties provide striking contrasts in an otherwise green garden. Sweet Annie has feathery, pale green foliage that dries beautifully and smells as sweet as its name. Southernwood (also known, inexplicably, as maiden's ruin) has a pleasant fragrance and fernlike foliage.

The graceful wreath at left combines two artemisias. The base consists of Sweet Annie, and silver king appears as a silvery accent. To make the wreath, wrap a wire ring with floral tape. Then make full mini bouquets of Sweet Annie, and wire them to the base. Hot-glue other herbs and flowers to the foliage: silver king, dried roses, lavender, blue salvia, baby's breath, and rose celosia.

Silver king and silver queen artemisia supply the background for this pastel Christmas wreath. Form small bunches of artemisia, secure the stems with rubber bands, and pin them to a 10-inch (25 cm) foam or straw base with floral pins. Trim the final bunches for a good overall shape, if necessary. Hot-glue the decorations to the artemisia: lamb's ear, strawflowers, and purchased angels. Make a bow of 1/8-inch (3 mm) satin ribbon, drape the streamers across the center of the wreath, and glue the ends in place.

Southernwood is a fragrant artemisia with a strong camphor scent. Its feathery foliage is an attractive material for wreaths, including this one, which has a five-inch (12.5 cm) vine base.

Form several southernwood sprigs into a bunch, place one stem of statice sinuata in the center, and secure the mini bouquet with a short piece of floral tape. Lay a short piece of brown or green yarn (about six inches, or 15 cm, long) under the base, place the bouquet on top, and tie it on. Clip the yarn ends. Continue around the base, overlapping the stems of one bouquet with the foliage and flowers of the next.

Basil

If we could smell colors, green would smell like basil—minty and warm, spicy and intensely alive.

Basil is native to India, Asia, and Africa. In India it was considered sacred, dedicated to the gods Vishnu and Krishna, grown by temple doors and dwellings for protection. Basil leaves were placed in the hands of Hindu dead, so that they could approach the next life with talisman in hand.

Basil found its way onto European dinner tables centuries ago. Today it is among the culinary herbs most adored by committed cooks, and is widely cultivated throughout Europe and North America. Basil leaves are the primary ingredient in pesto, that spicy green sauce that causes diners to cast their eyes to heaven, and have a remarkable affinity for tomatoes. You know it's summer when you sit down to homegrown tomatoes sprinkled with snipped fresh basil.

Basil likes full sun, well-drained soil, and protection from the wind. It's easily damaged by frost and cold— sow late and harvest early. It's a good pot herb. Set a healthy plant in your sunniest window—and approach the next season with summer's talisman in hand.

The fresh wreath at left combines green and opal basil, for contrasting foliage and flowers. Saturate a wreath base of wet-type foam with water, and insert sprigs of fresh basil into the wet foam. If the wreath is kept moist, it will remain fresh-looking for several days.

It will also be fairly heavy. This is a table wreath—the perfect centerpiece for, say, an Italian dinner. After it's too limp to admire, the leaves will still have plenty of flavor for a future spaghetti sauce.

Most herbal wreaths use an herb's foliage or flowers; this one uses stems. Most wreaths are round. This one, obviously, is square.

The base consists of two galvanized-wire squares of different sizes. Center the smaller one (which will be the inside diameter) inside the larger one (for the outside diameter). Secure them with string-reinforced packing tape: wrap the tape around the two squares, forming two "bridges" of tape, one at top and one at bottom.

Wrap sphagnum moss around the base—both wires and the webbing—to form a square base with a hole in the middle. Cut basil stems to the right length and lay them on the base. Run a piece of wire over them at top and bottom, and attach the wire ends to the back of the base. Wrap pieces of thyme around the basil wood.

Then hot-glue on the remaining materials: lamb's ear, poppy seedheads, bells of Ireland, thistle leaves, globe amaranth, zinnia, tansy, pearly everlasting, dusty miller leaves, silver germander, and allium flowers. Wire on a raffia braid for a hanger, and glue a few flowers to it.

Of course, not all wreaths are time-consuming projects. This one is about as simple as they come. Make full bouquets of herbs and flowers, and wire them together at the base with flexible wire. Then attach the bouquets to a straw base with floral pins. The background foliage on this wreath consists of dried pineapple mint and peppermint. The flowers include basil blossoms, anise hyssop blooms, celosia, yarrow, and pink statice sinuata.

Bay

LAURUS NOBILIS

The original wreath may have been a circle of bay leaves. Sacred to the Greek god Apollo, this Mediterranean tree was a symbol of victory. The heritage lives on. From laureate ("crowned with laurels") we get poet laureate and baccalaureate, as well as the formerly productive do-nothing who is "resting on his laurels."

Bay trees usually grow about 10 feet tall (3 m) outside but have been known to reach a towering 60 feet (18.5 m). In containers they stop at a modest four or five (1.2 or 1.5 m). They can be grown outdoors in warm climates but must be potherbs—huge potherbs—where winters are cold. Bay trees are notoriously hard to propagate by seed or cuttings. The safest course is to find a nursery that carries them and buy a small tree that seems determinedly alive.

Bay is known primarily as a culinary herb, an essential seasoning in soups and stews, whether Spanish, French, Greek, or American. It also makes excellent wreaths. Its dark green, leathery leaves make a fragrant base for other herbs and flowers.

Large, lush, and full, the wreath at left still looks light enough to hang above a delicate mantle. Wire branches of fresh bay leaves to an eight-inch (20 cm) wire ring. Then hot-glue colorful accents at random: zinnias, bee balm, boneset, strawflowers, and silver king artemisia.

Bee Balm

MONARDA DIDYMA

After the Boston Tea Party, when the American colonists had flung all the British tea they could find into Boston Harbor, they discovered they had nothing to drink. Happily, there was bee balm.

Bee balm is a North American herb widely used for tea by various Native Americans, including the Oswego Indians of what is now New York State. A thirsty colonist tasted the fine, orange-scented beverage and christened it Oswego tea.

The colonists sent seeds back to England, and from there the herb spread to the continent and eventually to Spain, where it was called bergamot, after the bergamot orange. Europeans drank the tea for pleasure and for the same medicinal reasons the Indians had: to alleviate fevers, colds, and sore throats.

Both leaves and flowers smell of oranges. The brilliant flowers bloom atop plants three to four feet (90 to 120 cm) tall, in shades of pink, lavender, purple, and vivid scarlet. All are magnets for bees, and the red varieties draw hummingbirds from miles around.

Bee balm likes moist earth and thus grows wild along stream banks and gullies, and on the edges of woods. It likes full sun or partial shade.

To make the wreath at left, wire together small bunches of betony leaves and mini bouquets of bee balm, and wire them onto a vine base (the one shown is honeysuckle). Cover the wreath in silica gel, and allow it to dry. Then hot glue dried accents at random: corn-flowers, zinnias, scabiosa daisies, and johnny jump-ups.

Scarlet bee balm flowers dress up a base made of another interesting herb: broom. The leggy, yellow-green foliage, which grows three to six feet tall (just under a meter to almost two), was at one time tied into bundles and used to sweep the floor, not adorn the wall. Broom has bright yellow blossoms in the summer and brown, shaggy pods.

To make the wreath, form a sheaf of broom into a circle, and tape it together with floral tape. Hot-glue bee balm flowers over the taped areas.

Boneset

EUPATORIUM PERFOLIATUM

Everybody was dead wrong. Native Americans, usually savvy observers of the medicinal scene, believed that boneset was an excellent remedy for coughs and fevers. The American colonists thought so too. Europeans drank many a bitter cup of boneset tea to cure what ailed them. (No one believed boneset set bones. In times past, a flue with body aches was known as a breakbone fever—hence the name.)

Alas, according to even the friendliest chemists, boneset has no medicinal value whatever. It's interesting that when an herb *doesn't* work, that's worthy of comment.

Native to Mexico and South America, boneset was naturalized early across the American South—so well that it grows up to five feet tall (1.5 m) in fields and pastures everywhere. Its white, fluffy flowers can add a delicate touch to herbal wreaths.

Some foam bases come with mirrors in the center—like the one at left. To make a similar wreath, hot-glue sphagnum moss to the base, then glue on small bits of boneset. Glue on other materials to fill the holes: globe amaranth, bits of yarrow, and ammobium flowers. Finally, add two Canterbury bells and a bow of wired ribbon.

Catmint

NEPETA MUSSINII

A close relative of catnip, catmint is less prone to send the neighborhood felines into flights of ecstasy. Thus, while catmint is less entertaining to have around, it's also less likely to be flattened by 10 pounds of intoxicated cat.

Catmint is a Eurasian native that has been naturalized throughout North America. It grows 12 to 18 inches tall (30 to 45 cm) and produces mildly fragrant, lavender blossoms. An attractive garden border, it likes sun or partial shade and well-drained soil. It's often planted near English lavender, so it can echo the somewhat darker hues of that popular herb.

Young shoots add snap to a garden salad, and the leaves are sometimes rubbed on meat to flavor it. The leaves also make a subdued tea that has been recommended over the years as a mild sedative.

To make the simple wreath at left, twist several small vines into a circle, and wire them together at the bottom. Form two full bouquets of catmint, and wire them to the base, with the stems in the center and the spiky blooms pointing to the outside. Add a bow made with two strips of narrow ribbon, one lavender and one green.

33

Cayenne

CAPSICUM ANNUUM

If the Devil serves dinner in hell, it is seasoned with seven pounds of cayenne peppers. The genus name is derived from the Greek word "to bite," and cayenne does. Too much will take your head off.

On the other hand, cayenne is an indispensable herb for people who want a little fire in their food. Native to the tropics and subtropics of South America, Africa, and Asia, it adds zest to Mexican, Indian, and American dishes that would be boring without it. The trick is to find the right amount for each individual diner.

The fruit of this foot-high (30 cm) herb is a widely respected herbal remedy, prescribed for colds, hangovers, and, ironically, digestive upsets. It is spectacularly high in vitamins C and A (assuming you can eat enough to benefit) and dries wrinkled and brilliant red.

The culinary wreath at left combines cayenne peppers with cinnamon sticks and whole nutmeg. String bunches of peppers on pieces of monofilament and tie them to a grapevine base, spacing the bunches more or less evenly around the circle. Then hot-glue cinnamon sticks and nutmeg in the spaces remaining.

The base of this unusual wreath consists of pieces of bittersweet. Twist several pieces into a circle and wire them together. Hot-glue bunches of miscanthus grass and red roadside grass around three-quarters or so of the base.

Hot-glue dried cayenne peppers to the bare portion of the base and around the rest of the wreath as accents, along with bits of heal-all, cockscomb celosia, and one Strawberry Fields globe amaranth.

This unusual wreath looks more complicated to make than it really is. You'll need about a yard (90 cm) of unbleached muslin, a yard of 1/4-inch (6 mm) sisal rope, and other, more typical supplies.

Start by wrapping red paper ribbon around an 18-inch (45 cm) flat foam ring. Cut the muslin lengthwise into six-inch-wide (15 cm) strips, and fray both long edges to create fringe. Fold a strip lengthwise—almost, but not quite, in half. If the edges don't meet precisely, you'll have longer fringe. With the fringe to the outside, pin the folded muslin to the base with straight pins. Fold the cloth back on itself as you go around the base,

creating pleats, and pin each fold to the base. When you use up one strip, start another.

Hot-glue the sisal rope over the edge of the folded muslin, to hide the pins.

Insert a piece of 18-gauge wire into the end of each cayenne pepper, and wrap with pale green floral tape. (To avoid burning your fingers, wear rubber gloves while handling the peppers.) Vary the lengths of the wire "stems." Insert the wires into the foam base in a triangular, "sunburst" pattern. Tuck some excelsior (shredded paper) around the base of the peppers, and hot-glue some extra, unwired peppers to fill in the bottom.

Curry Plant

HELICHRYSUM ANGUSTIFOLIUM

This herb is aptly named: its silvery evergreen leaves do indeed have a sweet curry scent. Plant it where visitors will brush against it, and wait for them to inquire after dinner. The leaves deliver what they promise: add a sprig to soups, stews, and rice dishes for a mild flavor remarkably like that time-honored blend of herbs and spices we call curry.

Both the foliage and small yellow flowers dry well, retaining their color and scent. The best way to propagate curry plant is by stem cuttings. So the next time you're in a friend's garden and think you smell an Indian dinner, ask to borrow a cup of curry plant.

To make the wreath pictured, form a circle of galvanized wire and tape the ends together with strong tape. Form a background of lamb's ear: wire bunches of leaves to the bottom of the circle and bunches of blossoms and small leaves to the top. Hot-glue other materials to the lamb's ear: curry flowers, globe amaranth, yarrow, strawflowers, and white salvia.

Eucalyptus

EUCALYPTUS SPP.

An Australian herb, eucalyptus is an old standby of floral designers. Silver dollar and miniature eucalyptus (affectionately known as baby euk) have graced more wreaths and arrangements than perhaps any other foliage. The leaves add color and interesting shapes.

But this Aussie once had more important things to do. The eucalypts (all 500 species of them) make up three-fourths of the vegetation on the Australian continent. The aborigines ground and ate the roots and thus managed to avoid dying of thirst in an arid continent: eucalypts store water down under.

To the rest of us, eucalyptus is a remembrance of colds past. Its camphorlike smell wafts from throat lozenges, chest rubs, additives for vaporizers—whatever means of delivery will alleviate a respiratory ailment.

The pink and green wreath at left combines colors and textures gracefully. Pin Spanish moss to a straw base, covering the straw completely. Then pick in bunches of German statice, pepperberries, statice sinuata, and celosia. Hot-glue on the eucalyptus leaves and dried pink roses.

This elaborate wreath is a major undertaking, but the results are spectacular. First create the base: draw a pattern on a piece of paper, glue it to a two-inch-thick (5 cm) sheet of rigid foam, and cut out the base with a sharp knife. After you've got the basic shape, use the knife to sculpt various levels. Then hot-glue on the materials, starting at the top and working downward, overlapping the leaves and petals in the same direction.

Green eucalyptus leaves define the contours of the wreath. Other materials include feverfew, tansy (note the individual flowers glued on the upper inside curves), rose petals, larkspur, zinnia, blue and white salvia, lamb's ear, globe amaranth, Mexican sage, starflowers, and hydrangea seedpods.

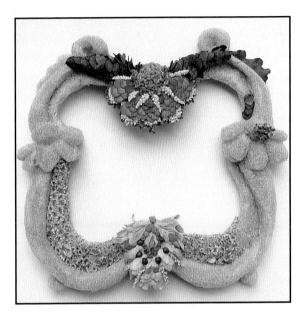

For a jaunty little wreath, attach a circle of dried materials to a straw hat. Just hot-glue materials directly to the straw: eucalyptus, freesia, rose geranium, and pepperberries.

Feverfew

CHRYSANTHEMUM PARTHENIUM

Feverfew is a medium-small plant with pretty, daisy-like flowers that dry well and enhance herbal wreaths and arrangements. More impressively, the British medical establishment says that feverfew's centuries-old reputation for alleviating headaches is well deserved. In double blind experiments, the herb did a better job of relieving migraine than many commercial preparations.

Plant feverfew in well-drained soil where it will get full sun or just a little shade. Bees seem to shun it, so don't put it too close to flowering plants that need pollinating.

The base for this wreath is a single wire ring wrapped with artemisia, which is secured with fishing line and allowed to dry. The base is porous enough so that the stems of the dried materials can be inserted directly into it and secured with a dab of hot glue: more artemisia for fullness, dusty miller leaves, feverfew, and roses (both flowers and leaves). A green cotton bow dresses up the wreath even more.

Below: If ever a wreath looked herbal, this one does. To make the base, wrap handfuls of mugwort (*Artemisia vulgaris*) and goldenrod around a wire ring, and secure them with monofila- ment. Make mini bouquets and secure them to the base with floral tape: double white fever- few, white salvia, yellow ageratum, boneset, and German statice. Then hot-glue individual flowers to the foliage: the centers of three Mexican sunflowers, hydrangea florets, zinnia heads, and burgundy strawflowers so dark they look almost black.

Below: This white-on-white wreath would look especially good on a dark door or wall. To make the base, wire bunches of artemisia, German statice, and green boxwood to a wire base. Then hot-glue on small bunches of feverfew and some white strawflowers.

Foxglove

DIGITALIS SPP.

Foxglove always appears prominently on lists of unsafe herbs. Many people have died after eating it—which is testimony to the dangers of self-medication. Ironically, foxglove is one of medicine's most valued plants. It is the source of digitoxin, used to treat congestive heart failure, hypertension, and circulatory problems.

Historically, foxglove was used to alleviate a host of ills, including epilepsy. As a side effect, the herb altered one's vision; everything took on a yellow hue. A common theory is that Vincent van Gogh used foxglove to mitigate his epilepsy and thus saw a world filled with brilliant golds and yellows.

Foxglove is a handsome biennial. Seed produces foliage the first year and five-foot (1.5 m) stalks of flowers shaped somewhat like fingers (hence "digitalis") the second. Foxglove likes a well-drained soil rich in organic matter.

Silver King artemisia and dusty miller wired to a vine base form the backdrop of the unusual wreath at left. Other materials are hot-glued on: a huge elephant garlic bloom at top to serve as a bow, lamb's ear, Johnny jump-ups, dianthus, roses, hydrangea, strawflowers, and yarrow.

Garlic

ALLIUM SATIVUM

"The stinking rose," it's often called, which suggests we're a bit ambivalent about this herb. Roman soldiers on long marches ate garlic by the handful to increase their strength and endurance, which may explain the Roman Empire: the enemy simply backed away.

On the other hand, some of the finest cuisines in the world would be nothing without garlic. It is an extremely common medicinal herb, prescribed for an alphabet of ailments, especially high blood pressure and heart disease.

Growing your own is easy. Separate the cloves of a garlic bulb (even bulbs from the grocery store will work), and plant them plump side down, one to two inches deep (2.5 to 5 cm.) and four to six inches apart (10 to 15 cm.). Garlic tolerates frost and cold; plant in early spring or, even better, in the fall, for a bumper crop next summer.

The easiest way to make a garlic wreath is to buy a garlic braid and dress it up. Form the braid into a circle, and wire the ends together. Then plump it up with additional bulbs. If the stem is left on the bulb, wrap one end of a piece of wire around it and the other end around the braid. If needed, hot-glue on additional bulbs. Finally, hot-glue garden accents to the wreath: sage, bay leaves, cinnamon sticks, star anise, and hot red peppers.

A is for allium, if you're into herbs. It's also for every other plant on this wreath. All begin with the letter A: small white ammobium flowers, artemisia vulgaris (commonly known as mugwort), ambrosia (the delicate foliage), anise hyssop, and ageretum (the tiny purple blooms). At the bottom are several large allium blooms (from elephant garlic), with a trailing "bow" of amaranthus.

To toy with the alphabet in a similar fashion, start with a straw base. Then form mini bouquets of herbs and flowers, and tape them to short pieces of stiff wire (let's say, 21-gauge) with floral tape. Then insert the bouquets into the base.

This imaginative wreath uses a pound of garlic, two yards (1.8 m) of muslin, and some odds and ends. Cut the muslin lengthwise into strips eight to 10 inches (20 to 25 cm) wide. Ravel the edges of two strips. Lay an unraveled strip on a 12-inch (30 cm) straw base, with the length of the material circling the base, to create a smooth surface. Pin the overlapping edges to the back side of the base with ordinary straight pins. Roll and twist each of the two raveled strips. Pin an end of each one to the back of the wreath, and wrap them around the base in opposite directions, so that they crisscross. Pin the other ends to the back of the base. Make a bow with extra muslin, and hot-glue in place. Hot-glue red eucalyptus leaves, garlic bulbs, and garlic cloves to the base. Finally, hot-glue globe amaranth and a few strands of Spanish moss at strategic points.

53

Goldenrod

SOLIDAGO SPP.

Goldenrod is a brassy announcement that summer is on the wane. Fields, pastures, open roadsides—all blaze brilliant gold with these spiky flowers, especially where there's poor soil, which the herb prefers. If you're not among the thousands of people who respond to flowering goldenrod with neck-snapping sneezes, this sun-drenched display is a fine farewell to high summer.

Historically, goldenrod was considered an antiseptic. The crushed leaves were placed on wounds to speed healing, and a tea from the leaves was thought to help inflamed gums and rheumatism. Actually, goldenrod is more valuable to crafters than to healers. The flowers dry well and retain much (though not all) of their warm, sunny color.

To make the wreath at left, form three bunches of goldenrod, brown roadside grass, and, if you have it, a pleasant herb called winter tarragon (*Tagetes Lucinda*). Position the bunches on a grapevine base, thread the stems through the vines, and hot-glue in place. Then glue on the remaining materials: marigolds, Queen Anne's lace, bay leaves, long mullein blooms, and seed-pods from a shoefly plant.

Left: This lush wreath combines goldenrod, burgundy rat-tail celosia, and lotus pods. Form bunches of goldenrod heads and secure the stems with rubber bands. Attach the bunches to a 14-inch (35 cm) straw base with floral pins. Hot-glue the celosia to the goldenrod. Place lotus pods in a stairstep pattern, and hot-glue in place.

Below: Even when their color is subdued, the elongated flowers of goldenrod add interesting shapes to a design. To make this full wreath, start with a straw base. Pin Spanish moss over the surface, then attach the other materials with picks: bay and eucalyptus leaves, baby carnations, amaranthus, artemisia, and goldenrod.

Horehound

MARRUBIUM VULGARE

Before cough drops there was horehound, probably the most widely prescribed cough medicine in history. (It was rumored to cure the bite of a mad dog, but no one took that seriously more than once.) Mixed with sugar and water, then boiled until thick, it formed a hard, candylike remedy with a distinctive flavor. The fact that horehound is still an ingredient in some modern cough syrups is testimony to its curative powers. The fact that people have come to actually like the taste is testimony to our ability to become attached to anything that's familiar.

This bushy herb thrives in full sun and dry, sandy, alkaline soil. It can be propagated by root division in mid spring, by seed a month or so later, or by stem cuttings in late summer. Since you'll find it in waste places all over southern Europe, central Asia, North Africa, and North America, you might as well dig it up and transplant it to your herb garden, where its flowers will obligingly attract honeybees to the garden.

To make the wreath shown, shape mini bouquets of horehound about five inches (12.5 cm) long and four inches (10 cm) across at the top. To each bouquet add some achillea and a sprig of globe amaranth, and secure the bouquet with floral tape. Lay a six-inch (15 cm) piece of yarn under the base, place a bouquet on top, and tie the bouquet securely, trimming the knot ends. Continue around the base, overlapping the stems of one bouquet with the foliage of the next.

Lady's Mantle

ALCHEMILLA VULGARIS

When this herb is grown at all, it's grown for its handsome leaves—roundish, pleated, and lobed—and for the dewdrops that catch in them. For decades those dewdrops were thought to be especially potent and were mixed into various medicinal brews. (The genus name *Alchemilla* and the word "alchemist" derive from the same root.)

But the delicate, yellow-green flowers are also very attractive. They bloom in early summer, when that shade of "spring green" is still beautiful to winter-weary eyes. The full, almost fluffy flowers make a very three-dimensional wreath.

This wreath could not be simpler. Pick mini bouquets of lady's mantle into a vine base, and attach a bow at top, allowing the streamers to float down over the flowers.

Lamb's Ear

STACHYS LANATA

If ever there was a lovable plant, this is it. It's worth growing for the patch of silver foliage in your garden—imagine it next to bright blue or vivid pink flowers. It's even worth growing for the off-beat flowers that will stop visitors dead. But its real charm is its texture. It's just as velvety, soft, and furry as its name implies. Bored, lonely, or sad, you have only to go to your garden and pet the plants.

This sun-loving, drought-tolerant perennial grows easily and spreads steadily but politely. Once used to bandage wounds, the leaves and flowers both dry very well, and are fine additions to an herbal or floral wreath.

To start the stunning wreath at left, make a small hook with a short piece of floral wire, and hot-glue it to the back of a 16-inch (40 cm) straw base. Cut some white fabric into strips about two inches (5 cm) wide, and wrap them at an angle around the base. Secure the fabric with white-headed sewing pins, as needed.

Apply the leaves in three circles. Decorate the inner diameter of the base by hot-gluing leaves at an angle. Decorate the outer ring next. Finish off with the center of the wreath, positioning the leaves so they cover the stems of the inner circle and overlap the leaves of the outer circle. Hot-glue a bow of French ribbon to the wreath, and use scissors to trim off any glue strands; pulling them off by hand can break a lamb's ear.

Larkspur

DELPHINIUM CONSOLIDA

Larkspur is a time-honored delouser—a distinction that will be scoffed at only by those who've never actually encountered lice. It's also a favorite of floral designers.

Larkspur air-dries easily—just hang a bunch to dry in a prominent place, and enjoy the lavenders, blues, and bright pinks. It propagates easily from seed and self-sows readily in sun or partial shade.

Although larkspur has a history of medicinal use, it is toxic when ingested. Children should be warned not to eat it.

Whether purchased or homemade, a rustic twig base can be an integral part of a design. To make your own, gather a plentiful supply of twigs (a good excuse to be outdoors on a fine day). Lay a handful of twigs going in roughly the same direction, and wire them together at one end. When you have a number of wired bundles, wire them to a rigid ring (see page 11) or even to a coat hanger that you've shaped into a circle. Then hot-glue your herbs to the base, leaving the lichen-covered twigs visible: silver king and silver queen artemisia, pink larkspur, magenta globe amaranth, purple and white statice sinuata.

To create a triple wreath that's almost entirely larkspur, start with the base. Lay three wire rings together so that the center one is on top, and tape them together with duct tape or packing tape. Then weave whole stems of larkspur around the circles, staggering them so that all portions of the circles have some blossoms. Hot-glue more larkspur flowers onto the base, filling all the holes, until the base is as full as you want it. Glue on the remaining materials: globe amaranth, zinnias, strawflowers, cockscomb, and lamb's ear. Finally, wire on the bow.

Lavender

Lavender is so distinctive that we named a color after it. This shrubby Mediterranean native with its spiky flowers dates back at least to the ancient Greeks and Romans, who added it to their bathwater. The British adopted the herb and its associations, and produced countless soaps perfumed with English lavender. Lavender does indeed have a clean scent.

Aside from beauty and bathing, lavender's past has been tied to disorders of the "head and brain." For centuries lavender has been prescribed for headaches, anxiety, depression, and insomnia. (Perhaps that's why lavender sachets are so common in linen closets, where they scent the bed linen.)

In an open, sunny site, lavender grows between two and three feet (60 to 90 cm) tall and blooms profusely in early summer. Since its many varieties cross-breed with abandon, it's wise to put in plants, rather than sowing seed.

White and silver contrast nicely with subtle shades of lavender. Form bunches of silver king artemisia, and wire them to a wire wreath base. Hot-glue lavender blooms around the wreath in a spiral pattern. Then hot-glue pale accents to the lavender: hydrangea flowers, globe amaranth, strawflowers, and small purple wildflowers.

Oval bases provide some variety to the wreath world. Wrap an oval wire ring with artemisia and Spanish moss, and secure the background materials with wire. Then pick in bunches of lavender evenly round the base, working from top to bottom. Hot-glue the remaining materials: pastel yarrow, globe amaranth, German statice, bells of Ireland, marjoram, lamb's ears, and rat-tail statice. Attach the bow of wired French ribbon last.

Lavender appears prominently on herbal wedding wreaths like this one because, in the language of herbs, it symbolizes love. To make a similar wedding wreath, attach bunches of artemisia to a wire ring with monofilament, then top-dress with additional artemisia, for fullness and shape. Hot-glue on herbs and flowers that add to the vocabulary of romance: roses (love), thyme (strength), rosemary (fidelity), globe amaranth (unfading); cockscomb, carnations, and baby's breath (affection); blue salvia (I think of you), and myrtle (health).

Marjoram

ORIGANUM MAJORANA

Love and death—marjoram has accompanied these since ancient Greece. Wreaths and garlands of marjoram decked the halls at weddings and funerals. If you slept with a sprig in your hair, you dreamed of your future sweetheart. A Greek bride and groom wore crowns fashioned of it. Marjoram was said to comfort the dead when it willingly grew on their graves.

Marjoram is much valued for its fragrance—like a mild oregano with a touch of pine. Still used in potpourris, it was once a popular strewing herb— scattered across medieval floors to release its pleasant scent when stepped on. Although some people find it too fragrant for cooking, it's best known now as a culinary herb, especially in the national cuisines of Germany, France, and Italy.

To make the wreath shown, bend galvanized wire into a square and tape the ends together. Also make a wire circle small enough to fit well inside the square. These will form the outer and inner bases of the wreath. Wire bunches of dried marjoram onto the square, and wire globe thistles to the circle. Then wire the circle on top of the square base. Hot-glue the accents to the base: boneset, curry flowers, globe amaranth, yarrow, bee balm, and mint.

Mint

MENTHA SPP.

Many a promising herb garden has ended up a mint garden. This is a pushy plant. Gardeners have resorted to all kinds of barriers—like sheet metal—to prevent their mints' imperialistic impulses, usually without success. The best course is to plant it in a container—a half barrel, a flower box—or try to appease it with its own territory and hope for peace in your thyme.

Aggressive it may be, but mint is a delightful herb. It scents and flavors everything from juleps to toothpaste and is virtually a synonym for fresh. It makes a fine tea and an outstanding bath scent: tie up some mint leaves in a square of muslin, hang it from the spout, and let the bathwater run through it. Or just empty your leftover mint tea in the tub. For centuries the leaves have been chewed to freshen the breath (or disguise a foray into the wine pantry), and mint is a time-honored aid to digestion—hence after-dinner mints.

All mints have square stems, and many have attractive foliage. Variegated pineapple mint adds a special touch of color and interest.

Mint is very easy to dry; just hang a bunch by its ankles for a few days. This wreath includes dried peppermint, mountain mint, pineapple mint, and horse mint.

Start with a straw base. Form bunches of various mints, and attach them to the base, either picking them in or securing them with floral pins.

This fresh wreath allows various members of the mint family to show off their finery: mountain mint, black peppermint, curly peppermint, spearmint, apple mint, pineapple mint, chocolate mint, orange mint, eau de cologne mint, and pennyroyal (a blood relation who married out of the family and changed her name).

The base is a doughnut-shaped reed place mat with an open weave (others would serve as well).

Cut lots of mint with stems about six inches (15 cm) long, and cut at least 20 seven-inch (17.5 cm) lengths of green yarn. Beginning on the inside (the doughnut hole), tie small bunches of mint to the base, double-knotting the yarn and clipping the ends closely. Then fill the outside perimeter of the wreath, and finish off by covering the center of the circle. Attach a yarn hanger, for a hanging wreath, or use your creation as a table centerpiece.

Pineapple mint supplies contrasting accents on this gold-toned wreath. Pin Spanish moss to a straw base, covering the straw completely. Then pick in the other materials: variegated pineapple mint leaves and flowers, tansy, acacia, heather, freesia, globe amaranth, statice, and liatris.

Nigella

NIGELLA DAMASCENA

Love-in-a-mist is nigella's shamelessly romantic nickname. While nigella's blue flowers and fernlike foliage merit a place in the garden, its seedpods are the real attractions. The seeds within, also called "black caraway," are added to French and Indian breads, and the pods themselves are much loved by herbal crafters, for their intriguing shape, purple stripes, and hairy beard.

Seeds are readily available through mail-order catalogs. Although nigella is an annual, it self-sows readily, so you'll probably need to plant it in a sunny location only once.

The huckleberry base of the wreath at left provides a good backdrop for the herbs and flowers hot-glued to it. Glue preserved magnolia leaves (available in craft stores and from florist supply houses) in evenly spaced spiral patterns around the outside and inside of the base. Add rice grass and then nigella pods. Fill in with roses, chive blossoms, globe amaranth, and feverfew, and finish with hydrangea flowers.

Oregano

ORIGANUM SPP.

Common oregano (*Origanum vulgare*, to some) grows wild in the mountains of Greece, where it scents the air and blankets the hillsides in pale lavender flowers. What it doesn't do is offer much flavor—either in Greece or in your garden.

There are scores of oreganos, Mediterranean natives that came to North America with the colonists and escaped to grow wild in the northeastern United States. After being treated as a purely medicinal herb in the U.S. for centuries, oregano came into its culinary own when American soldiers returned from World War II with a taste for Italian food.

Many species have no flavor to speak of. Most gardeners recommend the species *Origanum heracleoticum* for the kitchen garden. If you purchase plants rather than seed, you can always nibble a leaf before you buy, to make sure you've got a flavorful variety.

Hang a wreath of fresh oregano in your kitchen, very close to the canned tomatoes, and allow it to dry. The scent will inspire endless sauces through the cold winter months.

Start with an eight-inch (20 cm) oval vine base and generous handfuls of oregano blooms. Form mini bouquets of four to six flowerheads, and tie them to the base with yarn. Wrap the stems of the last bouquet with floral tape, for easier insertion under the first bunch you applied.

This colorful wreath combines purple oregano flowers with accents of a similar hue. Cover a straw base with Spanish moss, attaching it with floral pins. Then pick in the remaining materials: oregano flowers, dark red roses and dried rose leaves, pink and purple statice sinuata, baby's breath, German statice, and stock.

A table wreath makes an excellent centerpiece. Begin with a 10-inch (25 cm) foam base. Insert mini tapers into the base, then cover it loosely with Spanish moss. Hot-glue sponge mushrooms at strategic points, and insert stems of dried oregano into the base, varying the lengths and the curves of the stems. Since they're fairly fragile, you'll need to use considerable care. Hot-glue birds, strawflowers, globe amaranth, and a pomegranate to the wreath.

Pennyroyal

MENTHA PULEGIUM, HEDEOMA PULEGIODES

Flies, fleas, mosquitoes, gnats, ticks, chiggers—all are offended by pennyroyal in some way and give it a wide berth. This herb is one of the best insect repellents around, a fact that earns it garden space even if you're not taken by its rather pretty lavender flowers or the minty fragrance of its leaves. Crush the leaves and rub them into your skin when you're bothered by bugs. You might give your pet a break from harsh chemicals: line its bed with pennyroyal and make a pet collar from the herb.

There are two distinct pennyroyals—*Mentha pulegium*, the European version, and *Hedeoma pulegioides*, the American cousin. Despite their similarities in appearance, they are only distantly related (both belong to the mint family) and have fundamental differences of character that occasionally outrage them both. European pennyroyal is a decorative perennial that likes dry, not-too-rich soil; the American is an upright annual that will take all the moisture and humus it can get.

To make the wreath at left, form bunches of Sweet Annie and wire them to a grapevine base. Allow a few strands on each side of the top to trail outward. Hot-glue sprigs of pennyroyal around the wreath, working top to bottom on each side. Hot-glue mauve dried roses evenly around the wreath. Wrap wired French ribbon twice around the top, and form a bow to finish it off.

Purple Coneflower

ECHINACEA ANGUSTIFOLIA

A purple coneflower is no shrinking violet. These are big, brassy flowers: five inches (12.5 cm) across, with purple petals surrounding an orange center, all atop a four-foot (1.2 m) stem.

But they have hearts of gold. Echinacea ("ek-i-NAY-see-a") is one of the most valued medicines in history. The Plains Indians used it for snakebite, burns, and wound healing in general. It was held in such high repute that a respectable American drug company sold echinacea-based medicines until the 1930s. In fact, modern chemistry confirms an effective anti-infective in the roots.

But mostly purple coneflowers are pretty. They grow easily from seed, thrive in ordinary garden soil, demand only moderate rainfall and soil fertility, and produce a spectacular display from middle to late summer.

To make the wreath at left, pick bunches of fresh sage leaves into a straw base, and hot-glue purple coneflowers onto the foliage.

The echinacea isn't immediately recognizable on this Christmas wreath. That's because the burrlike centers of the flowers have been dried and bleached in a solution of water and household bleach (10% bleach), to add a prickly texture to the wreath. Working in the order given, hot-glue all materials onto a purchased huckleberry wreath that's been dyed green: rose hips, globe amaranth, ornamental peppers, German statice, the cone-flowers, holly leaves, and plastic berries purchased at a craft store. Then make a bow of wired ribbon, and wire it into position. Finish with a few glass beads on wire stems, available in craft stores, inserting the wire ends deep into the base and holding them in place with hot glue.

Sage

SALVIA OFFICINALIS

In the seventeenth century, Dutch traders found the Chinese willing to trade three chests of fine black tea for one chest of sage. The Chinese were inept neither in tea growing nor commodity trading. Sage was a universally valued medicinal herb.

The genus name *Salvia* comes from the Latin verb *salvere*, "to heal"—also the root of "salve" and "salvation." These days sage is valued as a seasoning for fatty meats and for other strong-tasting foods that will take its pungent flavor. Its leaves make an excellent tea; steep them in boiling water and sweeten with honey or sugar. Sage attracts bees to the garden (sage honey is a delicacy) and its velvety leaves dry well.

The delightfully fragrant wreath at left contains six kinds of sage. To make the base, wire bunches of mugwort (or another artemisia) to a wire ring. Pick in bunches of silver king and powis castle artemisia, to add fullness and shape. Then make mini bouquets of sage and pick them in: common sage, purple sage, red sage, big chief sage, clevelandii sage, and Mexican sage. Hot-glue on some magenta globe amaranth, white ammobium, and fuchsia spike amaranthus, as finishing touches.

One of the prettier sages is blue sage, also known as blue salvia. It appears as an accent throughout this book, but it deserves a wreath of its own. Wire bunches of it to a wire ring base, and allow the base to dry. Then hot-glue accents at random: zinnias, strawflowers, globe amaranth, statice sinuata, rice grass, baby's breath, and chamomile.

Sage supplies the background material for this full wreath. Form bunches of the fresh leaves, secure the stems with rubber bands, and attach to floral picks. Pick the bunches into a vine base and allow them to dry. Hot-glue on the remaining materials in a random, even pattern: bee balm, cornflowers, strawflowers, hollyhocks, German statice, globe amaranth, zinnias, blue sage, pincushion flowers, purple hyacinths, and mint.

St. John's Wort

HYPERICUM PERFORATUM

The supernatural history of St. John's wort is
a long one. For centuries it was believed to
drive out devils. With the advent of
Christianity, it became identified with John
the Baptist. ("Wort" is an old name for herb.)
Legend has it that the first flowers open on
June 24, his birthday, and bleed a red oil
in August, on the day he was beheaded.

Herbalists were familiar with the plant's
astringent and antibiotic properties, and
prescribed it for wounds and inflammations.
Although this wild weed propagates by run-
ners (a method that characterizes many an
invasive plant), many species transplant well
to the perennial garden. Others species spread
ruthlessly, which makes them good ground
covers but dangerous denizens of the herb
garden. Check with the salesperson.

The plant is cheerier than the legends that
surround it. To make the sunny wreath at left,
wire mini bouquets onto floral picks,
wrap the stems with floral tape, and
insert them into a small straw base.

Scented Geraniums

PELARGONIUM SPP.

Rose, citron, lemon, apple, cinnamon, filbert, ginger, lime, nutmeg, orange, coconut, chocolate mint, apricot, pine, peppermint—there's hardly a sweet scent that isn't mimicked by a scented geranium. No one's sure how these natives of southern Africa manage to imitate other plants so well, or just what they have in mind, but they're more than curiosities. They're genuinely delightful plants.

Use the leaves to flavor baked goods, jellies, teas, and sliced fresh fruit, and to spice up potpourris. With their clearly defined shapes, the leaves are spectacular when pressed.

Except in frost-free regions, pelargoniums are potherbs. They faint at the sight of frost. While they may summer outdoors, they must winter inside.

To make this fragrant wreath, start with a wire ring. Wire bunches of fresh geranium leaves to the top two-thirds of the base, and let them dry. Wire rice grass (available in craft stores) to the bottom half of the base, then hot-glue on the remaining accents: celosia, German statice, and strawflowers.

Tansy

TANACETUM VULGARE

This hardy European native has been naturalized through-out North America. In both places, it has performed a variety of services. A popular "strewing herb" in 16th- and 17th-century England, it was scattered across the floor to release its pinelike scent when trod upon. Its peppery leaves were chopped into bland dishes that needed bite: omelettes, sausages, poultry stuffing, mari-nades for meat. In colonial America, cooks rubbed the leaves onto their work tables to keep the bugs at bay. And its brilliant yellow flowers yield a fine gold dye.

Most of these functions are obsolete, although you'll occasionally see small bunches of tansy hanging in kitchen windows to repel flies. What remains is universal affection for the beauty of the herb. The lush, four-foot-tall (1.2 m) foliage looks like tropical ferns, and the yellow buttonlike flowers dry beautifully, retaining much of their color. They're extremely popular for everlasting arrangements and wreaths.

To make the wreath at left, paint a vine base with varnish, for extra sheen. Then hot-glue on the dried materials: tansy flowers, roses, cornflowers, German statice, thistles, zennias, preserved oak leaves, drumsticks, and yellow celosia.

This multi-herb wreath rests on a heart-shaped, 26-inch (65 cm) base of moss-covered wire, available in craft stores. Form 20 t0 25 mini bouquets about seven inches (17.5 cm) long, laying them out in the same order: Sweet Annie on bottom, then silver king artemisia, German statice, tansy, and statice sinuata. Wire the bouquets to the base, or tie them on with pieces of yarn to protect their stems. After the base is covered, hot-glue pink celosia evenly around the wreath, and glue an anise hyssop bloom next to each celosia. Hot-glue globe amaranth at random.

Thyme

THYMUS SPP.

Thymes are a low-growing, sun-loving, bright-blooming family of herbs. At under a foot tall (30 cm), they make fine borders and edgings. Their pink, scarlet, lavender, or white flowers dress up any garden.

Thyme is a much-used culinary herb that flavors just about any meat dish and inspires honeybees to make a gourmet honey. The diversity is remarkable: there are thymes that smell like caraway, camphor, or nutmeg, along with the well-known lemon thyme. Decorative varieties abound—from creeping red-flowered thyme to the orange balsam variety, with its exquisite pink flowers and citrus scent.

Make this small wreath while your thyme is in bloom. When the blossoms dry, their color fades but their fragrance remains. Wind long stems and leaves of thyme into a circle, secure it with fishing line, and hang the base to air-dry. In a week it will be sturdy enough to use. Then make bouquets of thyme about four inches (10 cm) long and tie them to the base with yarn, overlapping the bouquets until the frame is covered. Wire on a bow to match the color of the flowers.

This charming woodland wreath will stay fresh for days, because its base is wet-type foam. Then it will dry beautifully. Cut a 12-inch (30 cm) ring of wet foam in half, trim each piece to form half an oval, and hot-glue the halves back together. Pin fresh green moss to the upper part of the base, and hot-glue a piece of melaleuca bark (available at craft stores) to an inside curve.

Insert fresh English thyme into the lower part of the base, making sure the thyme is very full, so bare places won't appear as it dries. Insert a pick into the bottom of a novelty deer, and pick it into the base. Hot-glue more pieces of melaleuca bark to picks, and pick them into the wreath at lower right. Insert globe amaranth into the foam, including some of the dried foliage.

Woodsy accents set off this wreath of English thyme. Form bunches of thyme, secure the stems with rubber bands or floral tape, and wire them to a 10-inch (25 cm) wire wreath form. Hot-glue on accents in the following order: a lichen-covered twig, mushrooms, chestnuts, a silk wild-flower, and a bird. Or use any natural-looking materials that have interesting textures or colors.

Valerian

VALERIANA OFFICINALIS

The most attractive part of valerian is its foliage. The emerald green, deeply toothed leaves are striking. The curative part is the root, a tranquillizer of proven effectiveness, prescribed as late as World Wars I and II for shell shock. Scientific experiments have confirmed valerian's power to calm the nerves.

Which yours may need, if you give valerian garden room. Cats get loopy around it, and legend has it that valerian attracts, er, rats. (It certainly attracts earthworms, but for any serious gardener, that's good news.) Then there's the smell. The delicate pink flowers have a peculiar scent, usually described as "musty." When the foliage dries, it stinks.

In short, valerian makes an attractive *fresh* wreath. A good place for it might be the guest room. Houseguests will feel royally treated for a few days and then will spontaneously move along.

To make the wreath at left, make small bouquets of fresh foliage and flowers, and pick them into a vine base.

Yarrow

ACHILLEA MILLEFOLIUM

Yarrow grows wild in fields and alongside countless roads. This tough, hardy, three-foot-tall weed (just under a meter) is one of our oldest and dearest herbs. Its medicinal powers are legendary. During the Trojan War, Achilles saw to it that compresses of yarrow were applied to his soldiers' bleeding wounds (hence, perhaps, the genus name *Achillea*). More than 40 tribes of Native Americans found medicinal uses for this ancient herb. Even as late as the Civil War, soldiers used yarrow on their wounds to prevent inflammation and stop bleeding.

In fact, modern chemists have found that an alkaloid from the plant makes the blood clot faster, that one of its oils is an anti-inflammatory, and that it contains a relative of salicylic acid (commonly known as aspirin).

Perhaps because of its curative power, yarrow has long been associated with magic. It was used in amulets to protect against blindness and thieves, and witches were said to cast spells with it.

In the perennial herb garden, yarrow blooms throughout the summer, adding its fernlike foliage as well as bright splashes of color. Its flowers dry extremely well and are thus valued by crafters.

The colorful wreath on the opposite page shows off yarrow in its many hues: white, yellow, pink, and red. Attach small bouquets of blooms to floral picks, and insert the picks into a straw base.

This colorful wreath has striking vertical and horizontal lines. To make it, form bunches of Sweet Annie and secure the stems with rubber bands or floral tape. (This wreath has eight bunches.) Attach the bunches to a 12-inch (30 cm) straw base and secure with floral pins or with wire wrapped around the base. Wrap the wreath loosely with 1/4-inch (6 mm) ribbon, securing the ends with hot glue. You'll need about three yards (2.8 m) to cover the wreath.

Place three cinnamon sticks, ranging from 14 to 16 inches tall (35 to 40 cm), upright on the wreath, and hot-glue them in place. Lay several dried yarrow stems (minus the heads) horizontally and hot-glue them in position. Hot-glue silk pansies onto the wreath. Choose several yarrow heads (the ones shown were dyed orange and rust with fabric dye), work them around the base of the pansies, and hot-glue them in place. Finish off by hot-gluing a few pieces of yarrow vertically and small clusters of yarrow flowers along the horizontal stems.

Right: Bright yellow yarrow will turn a few heads if it's on your hatband. Get a straw hat and a glue gun, and go to town—with yarrow, plumosa fern, celosia, and caspia on your cap.

Below: Lemon verbena adds its sweet scent to this colorful wreath. Wire together full bunches of silver king and silver mound artemisia, Sweet Annie, and lemon verbena, and attach them to a straw base with floral pins. Then hot-glue yarrow heads and strawflowers in a circular pattern.

Index

ADDITIONAL WREATHS

Front cover: The herbs in this fresh wedding wreath are pinned and hot-glued to a moss-covered foam base. The enormous variety includes bay, yarrow, feverfew, anise hyssop, baby's breath, oregano, roses, sage, cockscomb celosia, horehound, tansy, and violets.

Back cover and page 13: All materials are hot-glued to a vine base: oregano, mountain mint, roses, nigella, yarrow, globe amaranth, allium, feverfew, tansy, blue salvia, larkspur, zennias, and celosia.

Page 4: Background foliage consists of cinnamon basil, lemon basil, Sweet Annie, and silver king artemisia picked into a straw base. Dried flowers are hot-glued on: hydrangea, globe amaranth, strawflowers, celosia, larkspur, blue salvia, and ammobium.

Below: Bee Balm